I0457290

This book
belongs to

_____

_____

To curious kids unraveling financial wonders.

Copyright © 2023 by Kelly Lee
Econ for Kids
All rights reserved
Visit us on the web! www.econforkids.com
ISBN: 978-1-954945-16-6 (ebook)
ISBN: 978-1-954945-21-0(paperback)
ISBN:978-1-954945-20-3(hardback)

What Is Inflation?

By Kelly Lee

Econ for Kids

Charlie owned a bakery that sold delicious cookies and ice-cream sandwiches.

He had a secret recipe to make his yummy cookies.

Cookie Ingredients

Flour
Egg
Water
Salt
Chocolate Chips
Butter
Vanilla

To make his bakery items, Charlie always bought flour from his neighbor Alex, who owned a mill.

Charlie's town usually had perfect weather for growing crops.

Summers were hot, but not too hot,
and winters were cold, but not too cold.

Charlie had always been able to buy enough flour for his bakery.

But this summer was different. It was very hot, and there was no rain at all.

So Charlie's town didn't produce much wheat, which is needed to make flour.

Last Year

This Year

Charlie's bakery ran out of flour, so he went to Alex's mill to buy more.

When he got there, Alex greeted him warmly. "Hi, Charlie. Good to see you! How can I help you?"

"Hi, Alex. Good to see you too! Can I buy 2 bags of flour, please?" Charlie asked.

"The price of flour went up this year," Alex said. "It was $5 a bag last year, but now it's $10 a bag. Inflation is happening."

Charlie looked confused. "What is inflation?" he asked.

"Inflation is when prices go up. There are many reasons why it happens," Alex explained.

Last Year

This Year

$7

$8

$5

$6

$3

$4

Charlie was still puzzled. "Why did the price of flour go up?" he asked.

"We have less wheat this year because of the hot and dry weather," Alex replied. "Flour comes from wheat, so we have less flour too. We have to raise the price of flour to keep our business running."

Last Year

This Year

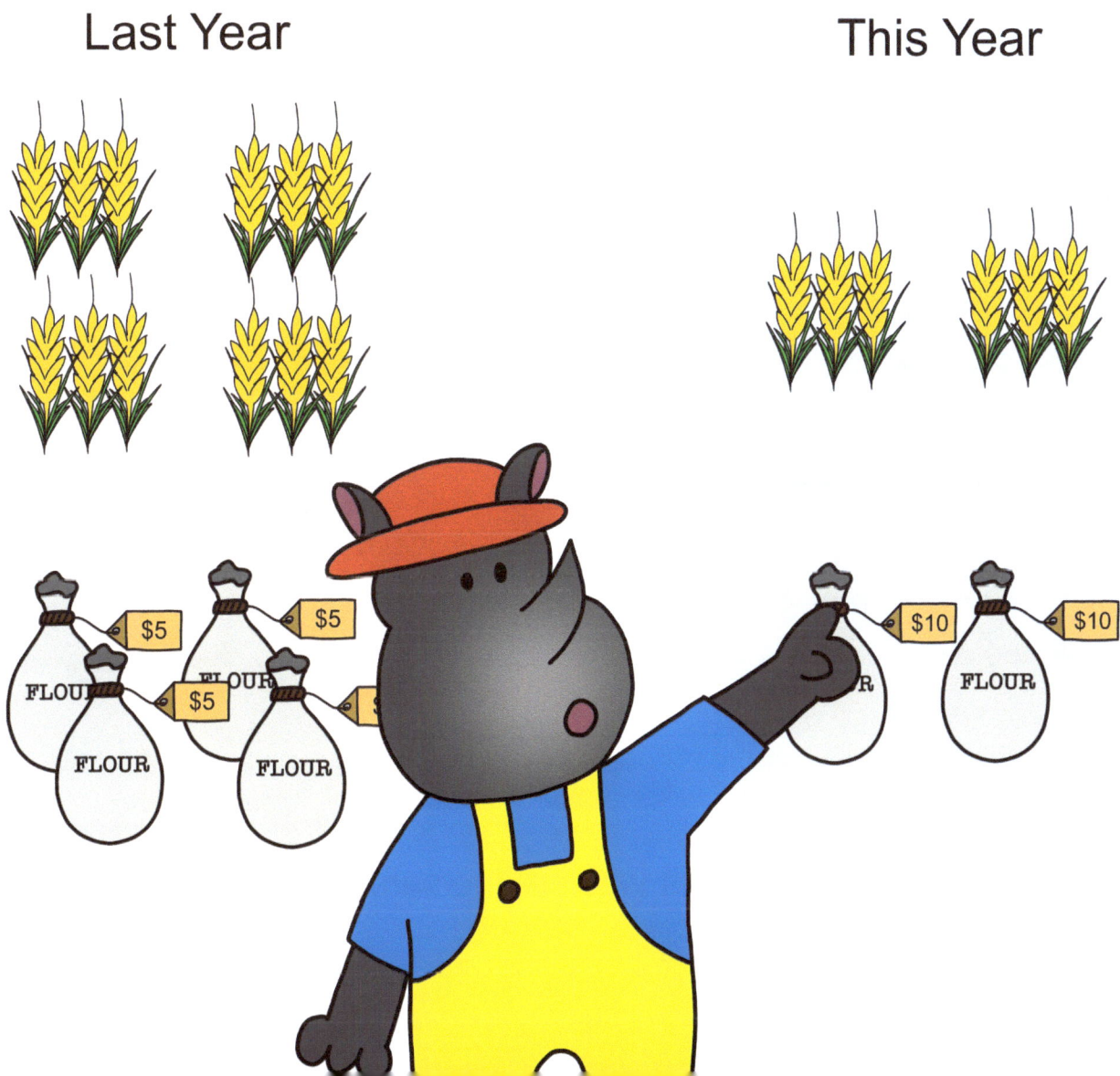

Charlie realized that he would have to pay more for the flour. "Last year, two bags of flour cost me $10. Now with $10 I can buy only one bag," he said.

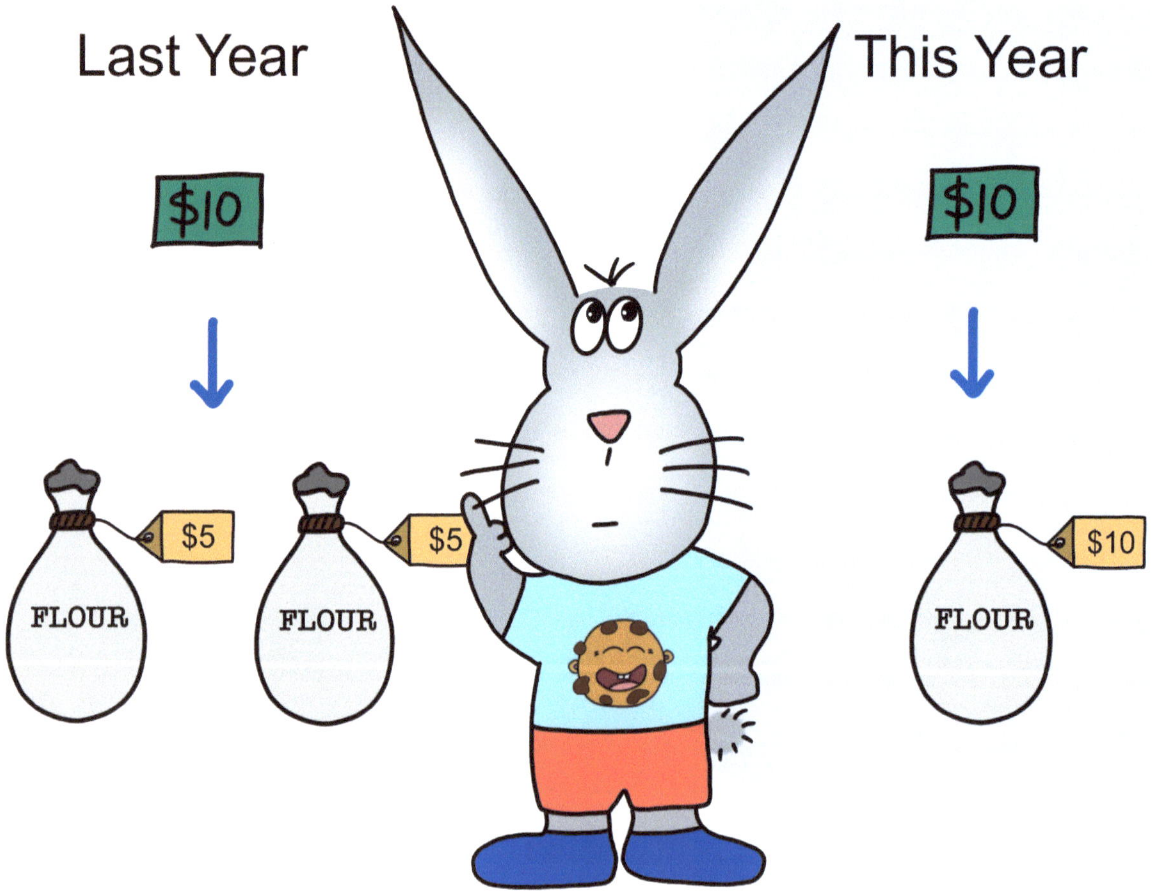

Last Year

This Year

$10

$10

$5

$5

$10

FLOUR

FLOUR

FLOUR

The demand for flour was still the same, but the supply went down, so the price went up.

Charlie bought a bag of flour.

"Now that I have less flour, I will have to make fewer cookies too," he said.

Last Year

This Year

"Can I still sell my cookies for $1 each and my ice-cream sandwiches for $5 each?" Charlie wondered.

"No, I would lose money if I did." Charlie was a bit worried.

Charlie decided to increase the prices of his treats to keep his bakery running.

Ava came to get some cookies.

She was surprised by the new prices. "What is going on? The price went up!" she exclaimed.

COOKIE: ~~$1~~ $2

ICE-CREAM SANDWICH: ~~$5~~ $7

"Inflation is happening," Charlie explained. "Flour is more expensive now, so I had to raise the prices of my treats."

"I have $2. I can only buy one cookie now. I used to be able to buy two cookies," said Ava, as she looked at her $2 bill.

COOKIE: ~~$1~~
$2

ICE-CREAM
SANDWICH: ~~$5~~
$7

"I hope the weather is back to normal soon so that I can change back the prices," Charlie said.

"Yup! I hope so," Ava agreed.

COOKIE: ~~$1~~
$2

ICE-CREAM
SANDWICH: ~~$5~~
$7

Dear Parent/Grandparent/Caregiver,

I hope you and your child enjoyed reading this book! Inflation is a complex concept to grasp, and this book introduces your child to the very basics of it. Our goal is to make them aware that the price of the same item can change over time and to help them understand some of the driving forces behind that. In this book, we use a simple example to illustrate how bad weather decreases food supply and causes inflation. There are many other reasons why inflation happens, such as increased demand, increased production costs, monetary policy, exchange rates, etc. These topics are fascinating but beyond the scope of this book.

Here are some tips to help your child get a better understanding of inflation. Note that younger children might not fully grasp the concept, and that's okay! The goal is to get them interested in talking about prices.

- When you go shopping or buy something online, take a moment to talk to your child about the prices of different items. Ask them why they think some things are more expensive than others, and discuss how prices can change over time.

- Encourage your child to ask their grandparents how much things cost when they were kids.

- Have your child pick a household item and ask what might affect the price.

- Go on a field trip: Visit a local farmer's market or grocery store with your child and talk to them about how prices can vary depending on the time of year, where the products come from, and other factors.

For any questions, suggestions, or any other finance topics you would like to see in one of my books, please email kelly@econforkids.com. Thank you!

Kelly Lee

Little Economists Books

 What Is Money?

 What Is a Credit Card?

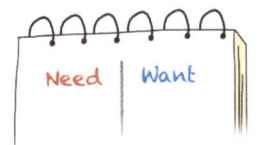 How to Spend Wisely

 What Is Supply and Demand?

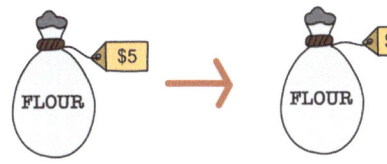 What Is Inflation?

Visit us at: www.econforkids.com

www.ingramcontent.com/pod-product-compliance
Lightning Source LLC
Chambersburg PA
CBHW041606120626
46551CB00002B/335

9781954945210